ABC to be Asth

Always **B**reathe **C**orrectly to stop coughing, wheezing and breathlessness

PATRICK MCKEOWN

Asthma Care Ireland
(incorporating asthmacare4kids.com)
Dublin Cork Limerick Galway Sligo Athlone

What do former parents of children and patients attending Asthma Care say?

"We can't believe the difference in our child and it's all down to changing his breathing. I would not hesitate to recommend this method to anybody"
Father of child with severe chronic asthma as quoted in **Irish Times** article "Help yourself to breathe easily" on May 25th 2004

"It absolutely is unbelievable. I have been on my drugs for fifteen years and to think that something as simple as this and as cheap as this and effective could be widely available. Everybody should be doing it. Give it a go, you have nothing to lose and everything to gain."
School teacher with asthma who was selected by RTE as part of their **Health Squad series shown on October 2nd, 2003**

"Before, I missed football, parties and swimming. Now I am able to do everything I couldn't do."
- Ten-year-old Lorcan, Dublin speaking on **RTE 1's Open House** programme on February 26th, 2003.

"Within a week, Lorcan was off all his reliever medication (ten puffs a day). He is now captain of his football team and he was not able to do that before. Before this, being present at a football match, depending on the wind, would be enough to start an attack."
- Lorcan's mother speaking on the same programme.

"I wouldn't get up in the morning without taking my nebuliser. I have not touched my nebuliser since November. I have taken my reliever inhaler three times since then."
- Chronic severe asthmatic, also speaking on the same programme.

"It's absolutely wonderful because it has given me a quality of life that I had thought was lost to me…I am absolutely amazed at how effective it is…. I reckon that if I live the next thirty years, it will save me a minimum of €12,000, but I can't put a price on the quality of life."

"Anyone who suffers from asthma, try this. I really can't emphasise how easy it is and how effective it is."

- Former patients speaking on **TV3's Ireland AM programme on February 3rd, 2003.**

My Asthma Free Book

David has asthma	Page 1
Summer sports Day in Tumbletown	Page 2
David meets Argo the wizard	Page 3
ABC Game	Page 4
How to unblock your nose	Page 6
What is our nose for?	Page 7
Walk the steps	Page 9
What causes wheezing and coughing	Page 12
Avoiding triggers	Page 14
The secret to breathe correctly	Page 15
The big race	Page 16
The Winner	Page 21
Note of Caution	Page 24
My Step Diary	Page 25
Useful Contact Information	Page 27
Acknowledgements	Page 28

Note:
The therapeutic procedures in this book are based on the training, experience and research of the author. The information contained in this book is not intended to serve as a replacement for professional medical advice. This book teaches the importance of breathing through the nose, how to practise simple breathing exercises and adopt lifestyle guidelines aimed at promoting good health. Do not change or alter medications without the consent of a registered physician. The author and the publisher specifically disclaim any and all liability arising directly or indirectly from the use or application of any information contained in this book.

ABC to be Asthma Free

First published in 2004 by: Asthma Care
Unit Six, Calbro House, Tuam Road, Galway

Web: www.asthmacare.ie
Email: info@asthmacare.ie
Tel: 00 353 91 756229

© Patrick McKeown 2004

Illustrations, design and drawings by www.globalsolutionsindia.com
Type Setting by iSupply, Galway.

ISBN: 0-9545996-2-4

All rights reserved.
No part of this publication may be copied, reproduced or transmitted in any form or by any means, without permission in writing from the publishers. This book is sold subject to the condition that it shall not, by way of trade or otherwise, be lent, re-sold or otherwise circulated without the publishers prior consent, in any form of binding or cover other than that in which it is published and without similar condition including this condition, being imposed on the publisher.

This is David. He would love to run and play with his friends, but he cannot because he has asthma.

His asthma causes him to cough and wheeze, and to become breathless.

One day, David sees a sign for the Summer Sports Day.

He makes a wish to be able to participate in the games.

His wish is: "I wish I could run a race this summer."

Later on that night, just before he falls asleep, Argo the wizard appears.

He whispers into David's ear: "If you want your wish to come true... you must play the ABC Game.

And the **ABC game** is...

Always
Breathe
Correctly."

The next morning, David awakes and thinks it was all just a dream, but Argo the wizard appears again, and this time David is awake. He reminds David that he did not play the **ABC Game** while he was sleeping.

David does not understand how to breathe correctly so the wizard explains it to him like this:

The **ABC Game**:

Part 1 is **Breathe through your nose all the time, both day and night.**
Part 2 is **Practice an exercise called Steps each day.**
Part 3 is **Always breathe gently and calmly like a little mouse.**

Part 1 of the **ABC Game** is to breathe through your nose all the time.

David tried to breathe through his nose all that day but it kept getting blocked and that made it difficult.

Then Argo the wizard appears. He whispers into David's ear the secret of how to unblock his nose.

You can try this too. Here's how:

- Sit down.
- Take a small breath in through your nose.
- This breath should make no noise.
- Breathe out through your nose.
- Then hold your nose with your fingers so that the air cannot come in or go out.
- Gently nod your head up and down.
- Do this for as long as you can.
- When you need to breathe in, then breathe in through your nose only and try not to let the air sneak in through your mouth.
- Calm your breathing as quickly as possible.
- Wait about half a minute and practice this again. Your nose will be unblocked by the third attempt. If it is not, practice this again until your nose is unblocked.
- If your nose gets blocked again, practise the exercise again.

Argo tells David that it is very important to breathe through the nose. Your nose, he says, stops dirty air from coming in and nibbling at the inside of your body. He also explains that the nose warms and cleans the air for us.

We all know that:
- We use our **eyes** for **seeing**
- We use our **ears** for **listening**
- We use our **mouth** for **talking, eating** and **drinking**
- AND we use our **nose** for **smelling** and **breathing**

So, breathe only through your nose because that is why we all have noses!

Each day, if David has his mouth open, Argo appears and whispers **"ABC"** into his ear...

- During physical exercise - ABC
- During walking - ABC
- At School - ABC
- Watching TV - ABC
- Doing homework - ABC
- Playing outdoors - ABC
- While asleep – ABC

After a few days, Argo the wizard is very happy because David does not breathe through his mouth at all. The wizard decides to teach David Part 2 of **ABC**, a game called Steps.

To play one set of steps:

- Take a small breath in through your nose.
- Breathe a small breath out through your nose.
- Hold your nose so that air does not enter or escape.
- Walk as many steps as you can while holding your breath.
- When you really need to breathe in, let go of your nose and breathe in through your nose.
- Calm your breathing as quickly as possible.

	David's steps	One minute rest	David's steps	One minute rest	David's steps	One minute rest	David's steps	One minute rest	David's steps	One minute rest	David's steps
Line 1	7	☺	8	☺	8	☺	9	☺	11	☺	12
Line 2	10	☺	11	☺	8	☺	12	☺	15	☺	13

David does two lines of Steps each day. Each line contains six sets of Steps.
After doing one set of Steps, he rests for about one minute. He then does the next set of Steps and rests for one minute until he has completed all six.

Each time he does the Steps he tries to get a higher number than the one before. Sometimes he can, sometimes he cannot.

Above is a chart of David's steps on his first day

Steps are fun... just like ABC. You can also play the Game of Steps.
Be sure to read the Note of Caution on page 24 before commencing Steps.

Argo has painted a table especially for you to complete. It is on page 25.

Each day Argo the wizard appears to David and whispers "**ABC**". Hearing this David repeats his Steps exercises.

Every time David forgets to keep his mouth closed, Argo appears and says to David and says: "Remember to **ABC**."

David is able to do more and more Steps each week. The wise wizard feels that his student is making very good progress. David is now ready to hear part three of the ABC Game.

Here it is;

BIG BREATHING CAUSES ASTHMA SYMPTOMS SUCH AS COUGHING, WHEEZING AND BREATHLESSNESS.

David knows he is big breathing anytime he can **hear** his breathing while sitting down or while he is asleep. David also knows he is big breathing if his **mouth is open**.

Argo blows a big amount of air onto David's hand. He tells David that this is big breathing. A dinosaur breathes the same way, he says.

Argo then blows a tiny amount of air onto David's hand so that David can feel very little air. He tells David that this is correct breathing, and it's just like the breathing of a little mouse.
Argo asks David to breathe like a little mouse, breathing quietly all the time.

Argo tells David the secret of how to breathe like a little mouse. David is to breathe like a little mouse anytime **he can HEAR** himself breathe.

To do this:

- Place your finger under your nose.
- Try to feel the warm air on your finger.
- Now breathe very little so that you cannot feel the amount of warm air on your finger.

David pretends that he is a little mouse. He tries to breathe very quietly and gently. There is no sound at all from David's breathing.

Argo the wizard has one final word of wisdom for David.

"David," he says, "if you ever see pollution or dirty air, try not to let it into your body."

The secret is:

- Breathe in.
- Breathe out.
- Hold your breath and walk away from the dirty air.

Argo wants to tell his secret to every boy and girl with asthma. He has written this especially for you.

He says:

"**ABC** each day.
Keep your **mouth closed** all the time during the day and night.
Practise two lines of **steps** each day.
Any time you can hear your own breathing, breathe like a **little mouse**.

This is the **ABC**."

The Summer Sports Day comes and David signs up for the race.

All the other children laugh and make fun of David because they all think he cannot run.

David is afraid that being part of the race will trigger an asthma attack so he runs off.

But Argo the wizard appears and whispers **"ABC"** to David. He encourages David to take part in the race.

He tells David that he will not have asthma symptoms if he can do more than eighty steps.

The higher the number of steps the better.

David practices his Steps twice a day every day.

After a couple of months David is able to walk 80 steps each time. He is now ready to race.

Below is his table of steps on the last day before the race:

	David's steps	One minute rest	David's steps	One minute rest	David's steps	One minute rest	David's steps	One minute rest	David's steps	One minute rest	David's steps
Line 1	80	☺	81	☺	82	☺	80	☺	85	☺	82
Line 2	83	☺	82	☺	80	☺	85	☺	81	☺	86

David runs in the race. He is halfway to the finishing line.

All the other boys and girls are running as fast as they can.

David wins the race. He is faster than all the other boys and girls.

Everybody cheers with delight.

Argo the wizard is so happy. David is great at running.

"HOW DID HE DO IT?" they ask.

David tells them: "I did it because of **ABC Game**."

ALWAYS BREATHE CORRECTLY.

- Breathe through your nose all the time.
- Practice Steps twice per day. The goal is to reach eighty steps.
- Any time you can hear yourself breathing, breathe quietly and gently just like a little mouse.

David tells them that **ABC**:

- Stops coughing and wheezing.
- Stops breathlessness.
- Helps sports.
- Helps teeth and gums because the mouth is closed.

David can now play, run, jog, skip, swim and do anything that he wants to do. His asthma symptoms are now gone...

thanks to the **ABC**.

A Note of Caution

Steps exercises are specifically aimed towards children and teenagers. While steps are a perfectly safe exercise, (similar to swimming underwater) it can involve an element of risk for some children with particular illnesses or susceptibilities.

Please note the following in particular:
- Do not commence steps if you have any of the following conditions: diabetes; severe asthma; epilepsy; sickle cell anaemia; any heart problems; a known brain tumour or kidney disease.
- If you experience an exacerbation of your symptoms, then you are not doing the exercises correctly and you should stop until you establish that you can do them correctly. If the child is having breathing difficulty, then do not do steps. Steps exercises are only to be practised when no symptoms are present.

What to expect

Roughly two thirds of those who apply steps will experience a cleansing reaction within the first two weeks. Cleansing reactions are indicative of the powerful physiological change which the body undergoes.

Children with asthma may experience excess mucus from the nose and airways, slight headache, diarrhoea, increased yawning, and cold like symptoms. Do not be alarmed if your child does experience some symptoms. This is simply their body readjusting to a healthier way of life. Symptoms are, in general, not disruptive and will pass in two or three days. Like any detoxifying process of the body, there is a short adjustment phase.

On a positive note, everyone will experience signs of health improvement including: fewer asthma symptoms; greatly reduced coughing, wheezing and congestion; increased calmness and concentration; better sleep and more energy, and reduced appetite and cravings for chocolate and other foodstuffs.

My Step Diary

Date	My steps	Rest*	My steps	Rest*	My steps	Rest*	My steps	Rest*	My steps	Rest*	My steps

* Rest for one minute between each set of steps
Two Lines of steps per day with at least two hours rest in between each line. Steps should be practised on an empty tummy.

My Step Diary

Date	My steps	Rest*	My steps	Rest*	My steps	Rest*	My steps	Rest*	My steps	Rest*	My steps

* Rest for one minute between each set of steps
Two Lines of steps per day with at least two hours rest in between each line. Steps should be practised on an empty tummy.

Useful Contact Information

Asthma Care Ireland provide special workshops for children at Dublin, Cork, Limerick, Galway, Sligo and Athlone.

Our **asthmacare4kids** programme teaches;

- How to unblock the nose
- The importance of nasal breathing
- Buteyko breathing Clinic for children
- Correct diet
- Asthma and exercise
- Correct Sleeping
- How to stop a wheezing attack
- How to stop a coughing attack

Freefone: 1800 931 935 for a free information pack.

Or visit our website:

http://www.asthmacare4kids.com
http://www.asthmacare.ie

Acknowledgements

I am extremely grateful to Liam and Anne Maher and family for their continued support and encouragement throughout every step of Asthma Care.

I am also deeply thankful to Marie Gaughan and Ronan Maher for their early editing of the manuscript and very helpful insights. Thank you Muireann Duignan for her assistance with proof reading.

Manish Shah of www.globalsolutionsindia.com has been instrumental in providing the drawings and design for this book ABC to be Asthma Free and for our adults books; Asthma Free Naturally and Close Your Mouth.

Special thanks to Kevin Kelly, who provided me with an accurate expectation of the trials and tribulations of writing this book, from the first written word to final completion. Kevin is best selling author of two self help books; How when You Don't Know How and; Life- A Trip Towards Trust.

To those people who willingly gave up their time to be interviewed on RTE and TV3 and the Irish media, thank you so much for helping to create greater awareness of this therapy. A special thanks to Yvonne and Lorcan Cooke, Elizabeth Mullins, Shane Fitzgibbon, Sue Emerson, Liam Lawlor (not the politician), Maura Coyle, Aoife Quinn, Anne Wilson and Jean McConnell.

Special thanks to Dr Andrey Novozhilov and Luidmilla Buteyko, my teachers, and to the greatest scientist of all time, the late Professor Konstantin Buteyko. Thank you for your undivided attention and for providing humanity with its greatest discovery to date.

To Sinead, the balance in my life, my partner and soul mate, thank you.

Finally, I would like to express my love and gratitude to my mother, father and brothers, without whom this book would not exist.